IT'S ALL
MINE...
BECAUSE
GOD
SAID SO

KENNYA HAWKINS

WESTBOW
PRESS®
A DIVISION OF THOMAS NELSON
& ZONDERVAN

WestBow Press books may be ordered through booksellers or by contacting:

WestBow Press
A Division of Thomas Nelson & Zondervan
1663 Liberty Drive
Bloomington, IN 47403
www.westbowpress.com
844-714-3454

ISBN: 978-1-6642-4680-5 (sc)
ISBN: 978-1-6642-4682-9 (hc)
ISBN: 978-1-6642-4681-2 (e)

Library of Congress Control Number: 2021920614

Print information available on the last page.

WestBow Press rev. date: 10/20/2021

ABOUT THE BOOK

IT'S ALL MINE... BECAUSE GOD SAID SO is a prayer book written to help you defeat Satan and his demons. This book is written to teach you how to fight in warfare against the enemy's daily tactics to steal, kill, and destroy what has been promised to you from our Heavenly Father. This book will help you activate the authority you have as a child of the Most High God. These prayers can be used by you, your spouse, children, friends or anyone in need of prayer. There comes a time in everyone's life where prayer is the only key to unlock a troublesome situation. Every day is a struggle for someone, either you or someone you love so why not pray your way through it by praying daily. I was inspired to write this book because I have experienced firsthand the power of praying these scriptures during times of trouble: for myself and others. I have also used them for times when I needed protection, guidance, and to be enlightened. Many of these scriptures were a road map for me in praising and thanking God for my prayers being answered as well. We are living in times where Satan is aware that his time is limited, and he has only a short period of time left to accomplish his mission of deception. As you go through this book and pray for the needs of yourself and others, keep in mind that the prayers of righteous person are heard by God, and he answers those prayers according to his will. It is time to get excited about reclaiming your life and freedom for yourself and for those you love. The only way to lose anything promised to you is to stop fighting for it. Therefore, it is particularly important to have a steady ongoing relationship with God. If He says it, it will be done. God is not man, He cannot lie (Numbers 23:13). We can always count on him because it is his will that will stand. The bible says, "There are many plans in a man's heart; nevertheless, it is the counsel of the Lord that stands" (Proverbs 19:21). I want to encourage you today that if you do not have a relationship with God, it is not too late to get one. This book of prayers will help you build a foundation that will get you started in your new or renewed relationship with God. The first steps are to ask Jesus Christ into your heart and then ask for forgiveness of your sins. It is as simple as saying these simple words which have so much power. He hears every word we speak and He is ready to work on our behalf when we ask him to come into our lives. If you are ready to receive him into your life, there is no time like the present moment. You can begin by speaking these words out loud I have written below. Once you have done this, He is in your heart, your sins are forgiven, and you are ready to move forward with your journey with the Lord Jesus Christ. Let him transform your life today, without him there is no other way. Speak Out Loud: "Lord Jesus, I recognize you as my Lord and Savior this day. Come into my life, here and now, I make you my Lord and Savior. Please forgive me for my sin and release me from all the guilt my sins have caused." In Jesus Mighty Name I give my life to you this day to live and act according to your will and purpose for me. Thank you, Heavenly Father in Jesus Name. You are now ready to move on to the next step which is praying the prayer of repentance and forgiveness for yourself and others whom you may be praying or interceding for if you are a prayer warrior. I pray this book will be a blessing to you and others who read it. Allow these prayers to change your life so that you too can be a walking testimony and witness of God's true grace and mercy.

PRAYER OF REPENTANCE AND FORGIVENESS

Dear Heavenly Father, I come to you as humbly as I know how asking for forgiveness of my sin. Lord I know that I am not perfect, but you still love me despite my imperfections. I come before you, asking for forgiveness of (speak the sin you want to confess before God) please forgive me Lord and create in me a clean heart (Psalm 51:10). Remove this guilt from me and help me not to do this again. Give me a clear mind and guide me into deliverance from this sin. God hear me as I cry out to you for help. Listen to my prayer. From the end of the earth, I call to you for help (Psalm 61:1-2). I am your child, hear me as I cry. Oversee my weakness and give me strength. Heavenly Father, I look to you now for wisdom, healing, and guidance Lord. I love you Lord and I thank you for forgiving me of my sins and for protecting me every step of the way.

In Jesus Name I Pray
Amen

BE ENCOURAGED

Once you have prayed this prayer asking God for forgiveness and you have repented, keep in mind that God has forgiven you and He wants you to also forgive yourself. Noone is perfect but if we ask God to forgive us with a sincere and humble heart, He will. He wants us to be free of the bondage of guilt. Guilt is one of the strategies that Satan uses to discourage us and keep us feeling hopeless and helpless. We start to feel unloved by God in which in return makes us feel uncomfortable in his presence. Our Heavenly Father loves us more than we will ever know. In Genesis 1:27, it says "God created mankind in his own image." God created us because He loves us. We are to never be ashamed to admit our sins to God because He is the only one that can cleanse us and set us free. If we do not confess our sins, it hinders us from moving forward, our prayers go unanswered which makes it impossible to clearly know what God's will is for our lives. As humans, we all make mistakes and fall short of our Heavenly Father's glory, but his grace and mercy are there to keep us and show us the correct path to take. It is easy to become confused when there is more than one option presented to us, it is God's presence in our lives that helps us to make the right choice. There are times when discouragement may creep in to misled you into thinking that there is no way out because you have not yet heard God's voice on the matter at hand. Please do not get discouraged when you pray about a matter, and you do not see the answer immediately. Please know that God is always with you, and He will reveal the answer to you in the right time. God's timing is always different from ours and He always knows what's best for us. We as humans are not perfect and that's okay because God is perfect. It is He is works on us and through us to carry out his will here on earth. There were imperfect people in the bible whom God chose to do great works through. For example, David was a man after God's own heart yet in the mist of loving God, He still sinned and had to ask for forgiveness. God forgave him and still used him to fight battles and win freedom for other people. Noone could defeat Goliath but little ole David came along with a single rock and a sling shot, killing Goliath (1 Samuel 17:50). Later, the same David went on to fight more battles that he eventually won also, but not before he started to get discouraged (1 Samuel 30:6). Instead of letting sadness and discouragement take over him, he started to encourage himself in the Lord (Psalm 13:1) and (Psalm 18:1-50) because he still had enemies like Saul, who conspired to kill him (1 Samuel 19:1-24). Although, his enemies plotted against him, he knew that if he continued to trust God, he would protect him and deliver from his enemies (Psalm 54:7). He trusted in God through every battle he faced, and God brought him out and he defeated his enemies. In the end, David was rewarded as king because he trusted in the Lord and never gave up during what seemed to be the hardest times of his life. If you hang in there like David did, you will also be rewarded. God is a rewarder for those who diligently seek him (Hebrews 11:6). He is the only one that can protect us from our enemies and give us the healing and guidance we so desperately need throughout our lives.

ONE

WHAT IS THE ARMOR OF GOD?

n this chapter I will explain about the battle we face daily. Some of us do not realize we are in a constant battle for our freedom. God wants us to be free of sin, guilt, depression, anger, sickness, disease, past hurts and more. On the other hand, there is Satan, battling every day to keep us in bondage by poisoning our minds and hearts with past hurts, unforgiveness, anger, depression and the list goes on. His goal is to keep us away from God by deceiving us and leading us into wrong thinking. Jesus died for our sins on the cross, so the penalty has been paid (Matthew 27:32-56). There is no reason for us to be constantly tormented in our mind and hearts about something that has been taken care of. Satan always has a plan to trap us so that we will not be able to move forward in our lives. He does these things little by little until his mission is accomplished. Studying God's word and using the tools he has provided for us daily keeps this from happening. We are to keep in mind that God already knows the plans and traps that Satan is setting for us, but we must seek God to know what they are. He reveals those deep and secret things to us (Daniel 2:22) because it not only helps to protect us, but it draws us closer to him. By building a strong Christian relationship with our Heavenly Father He will strengthen us and protect us in the midst of it all. We all know that it is difficult to fight something we cannot see but that is why God gives us his Full Armor of God. The full armor of God which is explained in Ephesians 6:10-18, it tells us that it protects us and gives us awareness of Satan's evil plots and schemes. Satan has demonic forces on assignment just as God's has his angels on assignment; evil versus good at hand. It helps us to have those spiritual eyes to see that what we are fighting with is spiritual principalities. It allows us to be guided by the Holy Spirit so that we will not be led astray. Satan knows what we like and desire to have just as God does but unlike God, Satan does not have the power to give us the real thing. He tries to deceive, so he sends something fake that resembles what God has for us and presents it as the real thing. If we fall for the trap he sets, it leads us to destruction. He has then done what he set out to do and "No" this is not a one-time thing. It is an ongoing process. The bible explains that we fight not against flesh and blood but against principalities and rulers of darkness (Ephesians 6:12-13). This is where God's armor comes in to play for us. When we are dressed in the armor, He has provided for us, his Holy Spirit goes ahead of us and shows us what roads to take, the traps Satan is setting and a way to escape or avoid those traps. Putting on all the pieces of God's armor is important because it help helps us to be aware of what is going on in the spiritual realm. These things can only be revealed and seen by those who have the Holy Spirit dwelling in them. I can recall making plans for things and right before the event was to take place, something unexpected would occur. When things like this would happen, God would already have someone or something else in place to fix the situation at hand. He would show me and speak to me the right person to assist me in the situation. He knew what I did not. There is nothing that Satan is plotting against you that God does not already know but it is up to you to pray and use the tools God has provided for you, then trust him to do the rest. It is important to put on the Full Armor of God daily because just as we change our minds daily, Satan changes his strategy to destroy us daily. He's very clever and manipulative and is always looking to catch you in a trap he has set. This why I cannot stress the importance of being watchful and praying always; leaving no room for the devil to get in. Our prayers can change his plans and he will have to flee. "Submit yourself to God, resist the devil and he will flee from you" (James 4:7). Prayer can allow us to take a detour if we need to (through God's guidance) and still reach the destination He has for us. Nothing that Satan does can stop the plan God has for you. Always remember to pray and stay focused on God so that you will be aware of what is ahead. You do not have to be spiritually blind because our God sees all, and He will reveal to you what you need to know to overcome the attacks of the enemy. It is time to let your faith be bigger than your fear.

PRAYER TO WEAR THE FULL ARMOR OF GOD

Heavenly Father, as I prepare to start this wonderful day that you have made (Psalm 118:24), give me spiritual eyes to see any traps that have been set for me this day. Your word says that we wrestle not with flesh in blood but with principalities and rulers of wickedness in high places (Ephesians 6:12). Only you know the unforeseen traps and moments of danger set by the enemy, lead me away from them. I ask that your Holy Spirit guide me throughout this day as I set out to do your will. I ask that your angels surround my mind, body and spirit to protect me from any attacks. As I put on the full armor that you have prepared for me, I know that whatever this day may hold, you are able to turn it around to work in my favor. I now stand firm placing your Belt of Truth firmly around my waist for courage and integrity. The Breastplate of Righteousness on my chest for a clean and pure heart, to stand for what is right in your sight Heavenly Father. I now strap down my feet with the Gospel of Peace Sandals so that I can stand firm on your word against the enemy. I place on my head the Helmet of Salvation for protection from attacks on my mind sent by the enemy. I take up the Sword of the Spirit, the word of God (my bible) as a weapon against the enemy (Ephesians 6:10-18) for your word is sharp and powerful as a two-edged sword (Hebrews 4:12). I ask that you spiritually blind the enemy's eyes and their spiritual ears death to any plans you have for me throughout this day so those plans will not be hindered. Help me to clearly hear your Holy Spirit communicating with me, guiding me in the right way to go. May my mind remain clear of any plans of confusion that have already taken place. I can now have the peace that you have promised to me, not as the world given, but the peace you give Heavenly Father (John 14:27). I also have the Shield of Faith provided by you surrounding me knowing that Satan's plans will not prevail, but it is your will that will stand. I am now ready to face this day with the joy, peace and blessings you have provided for me. May your peace reign throughout this day with everyone I encounter.

In Jesus Name, I pray Amen.

TWO

DESTRUCTION OF GOSSIP

Threbble tells us that life and death are in the power of the tongue (Proverbs 18:21) and that's why God wants us and others to use our words to speak positive things over our lives and into the lives of others. We as Christians are to build each other up in the word, (1 Thessalonians 5:11) and not tear one another down. This can be extremely difficult sometimes when someone says something hurtful to or about us. Our flesh wants to immediately get revenge by saying something bad about them but that's not the way God wants us to react to these types of situations. The bible says that vengeance belongs to the Lord, and He will repay (Romans 12:19), so we are not supposed to worry about getting back at someone when they say hurtful things about us. God already knows and He is going to take care of them. Although we are not to speak against them, we can pray about the situation at hand. Taking matters into your own hands makes it worse. Gossiping and speaking bad about others is a sin and there are a few verses that points this out to us. I have found out that in my walk with God, not everyone is going to be happy for you and some of them will not speak well of you no matter how good you are to them. These types of people have experienced pains, traumas and disappointments of some type in their life that they have not released to God so that they can be healed. When things like this happens, it is causes them to be hateful towards others. They do not understand that the problem is within themselves, not you or the people they are talking about. They also do not realize that jealousy, envy, gossip, bitterness and resentment are all some of Satan's tactics that he uses to keep them in bondage. We all at some time or another have been the topic of gossip whether we were aware of it or not. We are not able to control what someone else says about us, but we can definitely control what we say about others. We also have a choice on the receiving end of a conversation that leads to gossip. There Is a big difference when you are discussing something with someone else trying to find a solution to their problem versus talking negative about them to someone with ill intentions towards them. If you or someone else is doing this, it is important to keep it among those involved and state only facts. Facts can always be proven but a lie cannot. Gossip on the other hand is running with a rumor and basically telling anyone who will listen. The problem with gossip is most of the time when the information gets back around to the person it is about, none of what has been said is true and the person's feelings are extremely hurt, or their reputation is jeopardized. These people spreading the gossip are not aware that while they are planting seeds of deceit for others, they will reap harvest of deceit on themselves. Galatians 6:7 says "Do not be deceived: God cannot be mocked. A man reaps what he sows" This means no matter what you do in this life, it will come back around to you. The problem with people who gossip about others is they are not aware of the same ones who are gossiping with them will be the same ones gossiping about them later. Talking about someone else's business shows that the person spreading the rumors cannot be trusted. This is one-way Satan uses deception to carry out his will. His goal is to make others look down on you while causing you to be discouraged and lower your self-esteem. When you encounter someone spreading rumors and gossiping about others, that person has a spirit of jealousy on them causing them to secretly be angry with that person's accomplishments. In Genesis 4:1-16, jealousy led Cain to kill Abel his own brother and in 1 Samuel 18:1-16, we see that jealousy led Saul to struggle with evil thoughts that led him to commit murder. I mentioned jealousy here because in many cases it is the root of what caused the gossip in the first place. Gossip is demeaning and hurtful and it has even caused some people to commit suicide thinking that their life was ruined. Thinking they would never be the same because of these horrible things that have been said about them. Usually, the person spreading the gossip is very insecure within themselves and it is something about them that they do not want to be revealed. This is one of the main reasons they talk about others so that their flaws will not be pointed out. People like this are normally prideful and arrogant and they have no regard for others. Talking bad about others is their only defense. Satan knows this about them and this is how he uses them to carry out his will. On the other hand, we as children of God has the authority over Satan and those who are spreading the gossip. The bible says, "A gossip betrays confidence; avoid anyone who talks too much" (Proverbs 20:19). I can remember my grandmother telling me to always remember that if they talk to you about somebody, they will go back and talk about you to somebody else. I have found that to be true and this type of action displeases God. He wants us to be able to confide in someone we can trust, and that person is to be trustworthy enough to keep our secrets and we keep theirs. Proverbs 16:28 states that "A perverse person stirs up conflict, and a gossip separates close friends." Proverbs 11:13 also gives us an example of these statements "Whoever goes about slandering reveals secrets, but he who is trustworthy in spirit keeps a thing covered." It is important to live your life as an example to others. When you are confronted with gossip, the best way to handle it is to let the person know that you are not interested in someone else's business unless they are presenting this person to you for much needed prayer. This will allow you a way of escape to not be included in the vicious rumor this person is attempting to create. On the other hand, if the gossip presented is about you, you can let the person know (in a Christian way) that it takes two people to hold a conversation so you are aware that they have said something too and you would appreciate if he/she would stop speaking statements about you that are not true. This will normally bring shame to the one spreading it and turn their attention from you to someone else. When a person enjoys talking about others, they will always find someone new to talk about. We as children of God have a special tool that the enemy does not have; we have prayer. Below I have included some scriptures in this prayer for you that will silence your enemies and give you victory over them and their deceptive lies. God has a way of making your enemies regret what they have spoken against you, and others will see them and their lies for what they really are. No matter what it looks like now, keep your faith. God is only one prayer away. Let him hear your voice today. Let us now pray in agreement.

PRAYER AGAINST GOSSIPING MOUTHS

Heavenly Father, I come to you now on behalf of myself, (name anyone else you are praying for) in the mighty name of Jesus. I pray for an end to this malicious gossip and the damage it is causing me, my spouse, my children, etc. (the names of all the people you are praying for). Lord, you know who they are. They go around other people bragging and spreading lies making plans to hurt me and those I love. I look to you Lord Jesus as my/our defense. Let those lying lips be put to silence which speak proudly of things they know nothing about (Psalm 31). This was once my friend and now I witness how he attacks his friends, breaking promises and revealing secrets. Lord save me/us from these liars who plot to destroy others with the words they speak. "They were born liars from birth." "Their anger is as deadly as the poison of a snake" (Psalm 58:3-4). You who have a lying tongue, (the person who is gossiping) who love lies more than the truth and evil more than good. Who trust in your wealth and not in God. Who use your mouth to ruin the lives of others! Who plot evil against the Lords plans! Just know that he will bring your plans to an utter end (Nahum 1:9). You will not trouble me/us the same way again. God will take away that which you trust in; your wealth and lies. Then everyone will see and say, "There is the fool that trusted in his wealth and put not his trust in God." "He thought his lies would never be found out and his wealth would help him prevail" (Psalm 52:6-7). Lord help them repent of this and turn away from the evil they have caused with their lips before they are destroyed by Satan. Allow them to see the only way to peace and happiness is through serving you and doing right by others. Help me/us to not be bitter or hold a grudge against them but to be reminded of your great love and forgiveness for us. Your word says we are to forgive others and God has forgiven us (Ephesians 4:32). We know that we can always stand on your word even when everything else fails around us. Remind us that no matter what is being said about us that you are the only one who can save us and bring freedom from the enemy. We are standing on your word Lord, "Vindicate us oh Lord, our God and plead our cause against those who are deceitful and wicked" (Psalm 43:1). We are fully relying on you Lord to bring justice and peace to our lives. Heal all the broken hearts including (my own) who have been affected by this malicious gossip caused by the enemy. May our character speak for itself and may shame reign down on the enemies for their deceit. I love you Lord and I thank you being a refuge for us in times of trouble and silencing the enemy who is speaking against me and everyone I am interceding for. In Jesus Name I pray, Amen.

THREE

GOD PUTS PROTECTION IN PLACE

Protection is something we all need, and it is available to all who trust in God, but we must pray and have faith that he will protect us. In order to have God's protection, your obedience is required. We must obey God's word because it is what keeps us out of the way of danger. Just as our earthly parents have rules to protect us, our Heavenly Father does too. For example, your parents may warn you about someone you are hanging around because they are always in trouble and disobedient to their parents. Your parents see them on a path that is headed for destruction, and they know that if you are around this type of behavior, it will eventually rub off on you. In this case, your parents see something that you do not see. Our Heavenly Father is the same way, he sees and knows all. The bible tells us not to be misled or fooled because bad company corrupts good character (1 Corinthians 15:33). Your character is who you really are and not who you pretend to be, therefore it is very important to be mindful of the way you present yourself to others. If you listen to your parents, it will spare you and them a lot of heart ache and pain. Depending on the circumstances, probably your life too. No matter how old you are, you must always remember that your parents are giving you this advice because they have your best interest at heart. It hurts them to see their child hurt physically or emotionally and if they can spare you of those things, they will do just that. It is the same way with God, He wants to protect us from harm and danger. In order to do that we have to communicate with him through prayer. He will sometimes warn us of upcoming danger by speaking through a man of God, a person close to us or a funny gut feeling. There have even been times where I heard the Holy Spirit clearly speak to me not to do something. At the time I could not understand for the life of me why the Holy Spirit was telling me "No" but soon after I found out why. I can recall being engaged to this guy I had been in a relationship with for a while off and on. During this time in my life, I would always say a quick prayer of protection when something did not feel right, or a dream would occur mirroring a deceased family member, this time it was different. I had this feeling I just could not shake no matter how hard I tried. When you are preparing to marry someone, one of the roles of a man is to make you feel safe and protect you. I never felt that with him. I still felt this uneasy feeling that at some point everything would fall apart, and I would be left holding the bag. I continued to pray for protection, but I started to add more details to this prayer than just asking God to protect me. I started asking God to reveal to me if I was not supposed to marry this guy, show me in a strong powerful way so I would not have any doubt. God had been sending signs all the time but the problem with me was I was listening to people who did not have it all together them-selves. The decisions they were making in their lives at the time showed this. Things were moving along, and we got the blood test done and we had to wait about a week for the blood test to come back and then we would be able to go file for the marriage license. While waiting on the blood test results to come back, we went looking for the rings we wanted, we found them, but this uneasy feeling still would not go away. I can recall saying to myself that something is not right, but I cannot say what it is. I could not say what it was, not because I did not want to, but I honestly did not know what it was. He was in a hurry to make things official but the closer it got for things to take place, the stronger this uneasy feeling was over me. I started thinking more about the role of a man in marriage and the role I would have as the woman in the marriage and right then the picture still seemed to be a little blurry. I knew if I wanted this to be right, it had to be according to God's will. I started thinking about if he would always provide. Can

I deal with his anger? Will he protect me? Can I depend on him when or if things start to fall apart? These were just a few questions in my head, but I knew that they were a part of the answer to my prayer. I was still thinking I really needed something more solid and concrete that would be a way of escape so that he would slow things down and I would have more time to figure this out. The time came and we got the marriage license so then we had a year to get married and send in proof to the Circuit Clerk to have on file. I can remember him telling everyone (family and friends) he was ready, and we were making it official. It was going to be a courthouse ceremony. A few nights before we were to go, I can remember standing at the end of my driveway (at the time, close to the edge of the road) gazing up at the stars. It was such a quiet, peaceful, pleasant night to be alone and talk to God. Time was winding down and I needed confirmation quickly. As I looked up at the stars shining so beautiful in the sky and everything was quiet, I said "Lord, if I am not supposed to marry this man, please stop it. Send me a sign, please Lord because it just doesn't feel right." Well, I did not realize that this was it, the final confirmation had arrived. God revealed to me other plans He had for my life, and fortunately, marriage was not it. I must say it hurt but it was a relief. It was God's way of protecting me from a long road of heartaches and stress. God was not only protecting me from the present but also the future from a lifetime of pain. Even though I was not at the place I needed to be in my walk with the Lord, He was still protecting me in a dark hour of my life. You see God does not care about our imperfections. He is concerned about our heart and if we will be humble enough to pursue him in order to know his will and purpose for our lives. When you ask God for protection just know that He sees what you do not see so it is important to trust that if he says "No" it is for a good reason for it, even if you do not understand why. He says in Romans 8:28 that "All things work for the good of those who love God" meaning that something good will come out of it. Looking back on the situation, I can now see how this worked out for my good. In the prayer below I included guidance with protection because, sometimes God's guidance is his way of protecting you by giving you another route to take.

PRAYER FOR PROTECTION AND GUIDANCE

Heavenly Father I come to you now on behalf of myself and others in need of prayer for protection (name anyone you want to pray for). Lord, I ask that you guide us and protect from anything that is not of your will that may cause harm or danger in our lives. I ask that you remove anyone from lives who is envious or has evil intentions towards us. I am standing on your word written in Psalm 91:10, for our protection knowing that no evil will happen to us, nor will any disease overtake us. Give us wisdom to make the right choices in our lives so that we will not walk into any unforeseen traps set by our enemies. Your word says when we have wisdom, it guides us and protects us (Proverbs 4:6) from evil. Your wisdom will deliver us from those who are disobedient and delight in doing evil. We trust our lives to you Lord. Send your angels in flight now to war on our behalf as I pray to you Heavenly Father to create a hedge of protection around me and everyone I am praying for. Hear me as we cry out to you Lord on behalf of those I love, come quickly to rescue us for you are our rock of refuge and fortress of defense to save us (Psalm 3:2). Lord, help each of us to always remember that protection is granted to those who are obedient to your word and to those who walk uprightly in their integrity. "The integrity of the upright guides them, but the unfaithful are destroyed by duplicity" (Proverbs 11:3). Help each of us (myself and everyone I am praying for in this prayer) to engrave this scripture in minds and hearts as a reminder that you will guide us as we walk upright according to your word. Let the wicked fall into the traps they have set for us while we escape freely and unharmed (Psalm 141:10). I speak now in the name of Jesus that we will lie down in peace and sleep because you alone Lord makes us to dwell in safety (Psalm 4:8) according to your perfect will for our lives. Send your angels to watch over each of us while we sleep to protect our minds and bodies from any evil deeds or threats sent by Satan through dreams. May we awake each morning with a clear mind, positive attitude and a clear prospective about the things going on in our lives. Help us to see ourselves as champions on the battlefield for you Lord. I thank you this day for our protection and guidance and we know that even when we do not feel your presence at that moment, we can still be assured that you are watching over us to protect us and that no harm or danger will come our way. I pray that each of us will have peaceful sleep tonight knowing that we are protected from those who plot evil against us because you Lord, have already cancelled any evil assignments that have been planned. Our lives are in your hands. I love you Lord and thank you for your protection and guidance for us from all evil.

In Jesus' Name I Pray, Amen

FOUR

WISDOM IS TOO HIGH FOR FOOLS

The title of this chapter is particularly important because wisdom is what keeps a child of God from becoming as fool. A fool is anyone who believes that they know what is best for them and they do not need God's guidance to make decisions for their life. A fool is someone you cannot talk to about things because they believe that they have it all figured out. They don't realize that they are headed for a road of destruction. In my years here on earth, there is not a person here on earth that makes all the right choices and decisions in their life. Even the smartest people you know sometimes make unwise choices. In fact, many make foolish decisions trying to portray new images society say is cool or acceptable for fame and popularity; afraid of being judged by the world. For example, take a person with a higher degree of education looking for a spouse, the first thing that they would have on their check list would be the person has to have just as much education as they do. They make this choice out of fear of what the public may say if the person is not as educated as they are. They think that if the person has just as much as they have, they will live the "Happily Ever After" love story they have been dreaming of. This is an example of worldly thinking. Once this happens (as it normally does) they have the fairytale wedding, things go good for a while but after the honeymoon is over and the company cease, reality checks in that you were in love with an image/title and not the person for who they really are. When you marry someone, you are marrying the values that were instilled in them as child, you are marrying their past hurts, their mindsets (their way of thinking), their mental and physical health, habits, mood swings and more. You are marrying every part of them, and this affects your family too. This why it is so important that you pray and ask God who your spouse is to be according to His will because He will only bless what He joins together. Choosing a mate without God will always leave you miserable and in divorce court. Consulting with God and seeking his wisdom is very important for you because if you seek his will, He will give you the wisdom to make the right choice of whom you are to marry. God wants to be involved in our decision making because He is the only one who truly knows what's best for us. He always has our best interest in mind when he tells us what to do; even who to marry. He will instruct us on what job to take, what our career choices should be, who to keep in our lives and who to stay away from and more. The list goes on because God's want us to live with peace and joy in our lives and not be weighed down by sadness and misery. When we make choices on our own without consulting God first, we find ourselves in a world of chaos and confusion. Only God can give us the wisdom we so desperately need to make the right choice for our lives because He sees what we do not see. He is the only one with the power to take the most unexpected person, the person others are looking down on because they are not as educated, not qualified for the position or they do not have as much as someone else and use them for his divine purpose. God looks at our heart and our obedience to him. Material things does not make a person who they are, and education does not either. We must be wise in the way we behave and the way we treat people because God has the authority to take the shoes of the person you are looking down on and put those very same shoes on your feet. You may ask, "What do you mean by that?" What I mean by that is only a fool think that their wealth, finances, title, fame, and material possession will last forever. Every homeless person has a story that only the wise seeks to hear. The bible says, "Even a poor man's knowledge is despised" (Ecclesiastes 9:16). These people have knowledge that will never be heard by those who needs it the most. People you find that are homeless (not all of them) once had everything their minds and hearts desired but they did not seek God's word and his guidance. They did not feed the homeless when it was in their power to do it. Instead, these people walk by (no doubt) with their nose up, heads held high, and holding tightly to their purses or wallets. Some go as far as to lock their doors or even pressed down harder on the accelerator of their new car when they encounter the homeless. Only a fool would pass by someone in need. The bible tells us that the poor will always be among us Matthew 26:11. Wisdom helps us to see things the way God's wants us to see things through his eyes. I get excited at the thought of his wisdom and the way he uses others to carry out his will. Throughout the bible God gave those who were obedient to him the wisdom to win battles, lead nations out of bondage, the power to heal the sick and wisdom to know when to hide from their enemies. Wisdom gave David the knowledge of when and where to run when Saul and his army was after him. We need wisdom to know what battles to fight and which ones to avoid or run away from. King Solomon asked God for wisdom because he knew it was important in order to lead the people according to God's will. He knew that wisdom was more important than the treasures of this world because treasure is useless if you do not have wisdom to make the right decisions on what to do with it or how to spend it. Yes, wisdom can keep you from buying something you will regret later. For example, you can buy a house that looks like the dream home you have been praying about, without wisdom and discernment of God's will, this could be a trick of Satan. Let's say you get this house and once you get in, you find out that all the pipes are old and need to be replaced, the wiring in the home is faulty and needs rewiring and the floors are dry rotted under the carpet. Wow! Imagine that you have bought your dream nightmare instead. God's wisdom and guidance would have made you aware of this. There would have been a feeling that something is not right with this home. When we have wisdom from our Heavenly Father, it will lead us to make the right purchases, choose the right jobs and put us in line with people who will help promote us on our journey of life. God calls unqualified and put them in places that others say they are not qualified for because they do not have the degree or experience. In the scripture it says, "God chose the foolish things of the world to shame the wise; God chose the weak things of the world to shame the strong" 1 Corinthians 1:27, this means worldly wisdom and strength means nothing if you do not have God in your life. It is impossible to live a happy life without the one who created you. God does not want us think that just because we do not have as much education as the world think we should have or as the next person that does not mean that God cannot still use you to carry out his purpose for your life. It is time for you to see yourself the way God sees you and pursue his wisdom for your life. It is never too late to ask God for wisdom for your life. The choices and decisions you make affects everyone associated with you; even those praying for you. Wisdom, God's wisdom can change your life forever. Through his wisdom you can receive his grace and mercy for any wrong decisions you have already made. Trust him with any decision you must make. God has the authority to put you in that position you are desiring but do not think you are qualified for. Don't worry about it, because when God puts you in the position, he will give you the wisdom, knowledge and courage to complete every task thrown your way. When God positions you for a thing, he sends his Holy Spirit to help you excel so that it will show others that He is almighty and there is no other god like him. Just remember when He gives you everything your heart desires, give him the glory because without him you could not have done it.

PRAYER FOR WISDOM

Heavenly Father, I am coming to you now with a humble heart and a cloudy mind. Lord, I have a decision to make in my life and I am not sure of how to handle it or the best route to take. I am leaning and depending on you. I know that wisdom of the world is foolish in the sight of you because no one knows your plan or purpose for my life. The decision I must make is (tell God about whatever the decision(s) is that you must make). In the past, I have searched for wisdom from others who were not following you and it caused me to take the exit off the path you had for me. I had to live with some serious consequences because of this disobedience in seeking the opinion of others instead of yours. I have learned from those mistakes Lord and I am ready to depend completely on your wisdom and guidance for my life. I know only you know what is best for me and I want what you want for me. Only your infinite wisdom and guidance can bring clarity to my mind and peace in my life. Deliver me from any disobedience that will cause me to go astray and not hear voice. Give me wisdom of when to speak and when not to speak, your word clearly states that "Even fools are thought to be wise if they keep silent and discerning if they hold their tongues" (Proverbs 17:28). I do not ever want to be a fool. I also ask that you give me the wisdom and knowledge I need when choosing the right spouse for my life as well. I know that making the right choice is important, because it can have a great impact on my children and the purpose you have for my life. Reveal to me the spouse you have for me and give both of us the wisdom and knowledge to recognize each other when we meet. Help both of us to seek your guidance and wisdom throughout the relationship and marriage. Show us who to associate with and who to stay away from that would cause trouble between us. Any friendship I have Lord that is not part of your will and purpose for my life make me aware of it and give me the wisdom and knowledge I need to sever the relationship. I know that being connected to the wrong people will cause me to think like the crowd and it will affect the outcome you have for my life. Give me wisdom in every area of my life, even in my career choices so that I will not be led into destruction because of foolish decisions. Help me to always seek your will first for any decisions I have to make in my life, no matter how big or small. I know that even the smallest decision today can have the greatest impact on my life tomorrow as well as the lives of others close to me. Give them wisdom too so that they can make wise choices in their own lives. Lord be with me every step of the way and let your word be my guiding light. I love you Lord and I thank you in advance for the wisdom you have in store for me.

In Jesus Name I Pray, Amen

FIVE

THEY HAVE ALREADY PAID THE PRICE (VETERANS)

n this chapter I really wanted to focus on our Veterans. Our military soldiers are trained physically for battle, but in many cases, they are not trained mentally, the battle of their mind. We see them as strong individuals prepared to fight and protect us, but no one stops to think about once they are home and the physical battle is over, that this is when the spiritual battle begins. Satan has already prepared his demons to send them out on assignment to attack their minds. I have witnessed this more times than I can list here in this book from being a caregiver, to having relatives who were retired military veterans, to friends in the military and each of their experiences were very similar. I felt like God prompted this on my heart because while prayer does not change what they have already went through, it can help them heal from their emotional wounds and detour the attacks sent against their minds. It appeared to me that as I am currently writing this chapter it is a few days shy of Veterans Day. Wow! What a confirmation wouldn't you say? While some may be preparing to celebrate Veterans Day, my focus is making others aware of what they may be going through as they prepare to put on a smile to thank others for recognizing them on this national day set aside for the great work they have done. Although many of them may be smiling with joy on the outside, they are battling hurt, fear, loneliness and depression on the inside. It's easy to look at a person and say, "Oh he or she is ok, they have everything they need" but sometimes what a person really needs is something you cannot see, and prayer is the key to bring that something on the scene they need. Most people who have served in the military experience loneliness and detachment from others because of the fear of being judged and not knowing who they can trust and depend on. There is always a negative thought that Satan sends to make them believe that they can only trust a few people out of fear of being betrayed. Satan hates godly relationships because he knows that those relationships bring healing and reverses those negative thoughts. This why it's important to be around people who have a positive effect on you. Ungodly friendships bring chaos and destruction because they are not listening for the voice of God but rather are following their own worldly ways. If a person's mind is cloudy, it makes it difficult to focus and think clearly. It impossible to separate the truth from what is false without much needed prayer along with divine confirmation from God. God wants us to pray for others to know the truth because that is the only way to be completely free. Without prayer, the tormenting memories of their past experiences will follow them, and this is exactly what Satan needs to administer his attack. You have the authority not to let that happen. God gives us the authority to trample on serpents and scorpions and nothing will by any means hurt us so there is no need to fear. Satan uses fear also as his weapon of defense. I have noticed with some elderly patients I have cared for in the past that have fought in World War I and World War II relives those events in their mind. In some cases, they have fought back and acted out. This happens when they reach a certain age and diseases like Dementia and Alzheimer's set in. When this takes place, the mind and the body are in two different places. Let me explain, the body is home physically in that moment, but the mind has gone back to the traumatic events of their past that happened so many years ago. In their mind, they are fighting for their life so everyone they encounter is an enemy and they are in danger. They do not mean to harm you, but they do not understand that their mind is being spiritually attacked and they have no control over what is going on in that moment. Therefore, I feel that it is important to start prayer early for them to stop this attack from taking place. There may be times when your spouse or loved one may not say anything, but you can sense that something is wrong. It is important to pay attention to this because one of the signs that a spiritual attack is taking place is silence and rejection. The person you seemed so close to 20 years ago may wake up today and make you feel like a stranger in your own home. This is because Satan has reminded them of what happened and told them that you and no one else will understand and that they will be judged and talked about in the worse way. Although this is certainly not true, Satan lies can become convincing even to someone who believes in God but is not spiritually strong enough to reject the lies being told to them. Our minds are very fragile, and Satan knows that. Where your mind goes, your body will eventually follow. This is the main reason for the attack on the mind first. If you are a spouse reading this, do not give up on your marriage because this is the time, he or she needs you the most. The prayers of a righteous wife are heard and answered and vice versa for the husband. You two are one, a union united under the covenant of God so what affects him or her, affects you also. This also applies to mothers if your child is a veteran and whether they have started experiencing some of these signs or not, it is very important to start praying now because Satan has a plan and a set time for his attack. He likes to take us by surprise but with the word of God present and prayer, you can be prepared because nothing catches God by surprise. Deuteronomy 29:29 says that "The secret things belong to the Lord our God, but the things revealed belong to us and to our children forever, that we may follow all the words of the law." God wants us to know the planned attacks ahead of time. The prayers in the other chapters of this book can also be used for them. As a matter of fact, I would advise you to pray those for them anyway, do not leave your loved ones uncovered. The prayer below can be used to pray for anyone who is active in the military or no longer active in the military. Pray for anyone who comes to mind, you never know why God placed them on your heart. There are some people who do not know how to pray for themselves and there is nothing wrong with that. That is why God wants us to be prayer warriors so that we can intercede on their behalf. On the other hand, you have some people who know how to pray and what it means to pray but they are not able to pray for themselves because the attack on their mind is so strong that it causes them to lose their focus on God and their faith. This chapter really touches me as I write it because there are many Veterans who are currently sitting in their homes fighting spiritually for the freedom of their minds and the hopes of living a life they can truly enjoy. Let's start now to touch and agree in prayer for the Veterans in our lives. They need us more that we will ever know. May God bless you for taking the time out to give those who mean so much to us and others the gift of prayer that can change their lives for the better. When you pray for others, you are showing the love of God in your heart for them. You are also trusting that God will take care of them in ways you cannot without prayer. He is all powerful and all knowing. Make your request known to him so that he can fix and mend what is broken.

PRAYER FOR HEALING
FOR OUR VETERANS

Heavenly Father, I come to you now in the mighty name of Jesus on behalf of every veteran in my life today. I especially want to pray for (speak person(s) name you're praying for). Protect them in all their ways and in everything they do. Give them clarity for their thoughts and a clear mind and heart. Send your angels to surround and protect them from Satan's evil plans to destroy their lives. I know that nothing is impossible with you God, so I ask that you cover them with the blood of Jesus and that no assaults or attacks (spiritually, mentally or physically) will be able to come their way. I know that the battle they are facing is daily, so I ask that you send your angels in flight to surround and protect them. Let no weapon formed against them be able to prosper (Isaiah 54:17). Deliver (speak the persons' name) from those tormenting memories of their past that has caused destruction in their lives. Heal them Lord of any sickness or disease in their body that has been brought on by any satanic attack. I speak right now in the name of Jesus to the root of the illness (name the root cause of it if you know it) to be uprooted now. Depression you must go, anxiety you must now flee. (Speak the person's name) is a child of the Most High God. Mental illness you have visited long enough, your time is up, this is not a place for you to call home. You are now fleeing in the Mighty Name of Jesus. PTSD you were left behind in the battle years ago. You are now part of (the person's name) past and you are no longer welcome in their life. I decree that (speak the person's name) is now delivered from their past and the tormenting memories that have held them captive by Satan and his army are no longer present. They have been released. Satan you no longer have any control over their lives. I decree and declare that right now in the Mighty Name of Jesus that (speak the person's name) body is the temple of the Lord and is filled with the fruits of the Holy Spirit, which is love, joy, peace, patience, kindness, gentleness, meekness, faithfulness and self-control (Galatians 5:22-23). Therefore, (speak the person's name) no longer has room for anger, bitterness, anxiety, resentment, pride, sadness, rejection, depression, impatience, chaos or destruction their lives. These demonic spirits no longer have a home in (speak the person's name) mind and body in the Name of Jesus. I speak right now in the name of Jesus that any illness that these demonic spirits have caused in (speak the person's name) mind and body is cast out and sent into outer darkness along with these demonic spirits. They will no longer be able to harm or hurt them anymore and they will now be free to live the life God created for them. No longer will destruction and chaos be allowed to control their mind in any way. I decree and declare that from this day forward, (Speak the person's name) is now free to live a happy and prosperous life. They are now ready to serve the Lord with their whole heart. Thank you, Lord, for giving them the freedom they so long for and bringing them out of darkness back to your marvelous light. They are no longer victims of Satan but Victors of Jesus Christ. Lord, help them to always remember that your son Jesus died on the cross for their sins, and they have already been forgiven when Satan tries to remind them of anything you have forgiven and delivered them from. Lord you said in your word that we are to submit to you and resist the devil and he will flee from us (James 4:7), help (speak the person's name) to continue to do that from this day forward. Speak to me Holy Spirit if I am to pray this prayer again in the future because Satan is plotting an attack on someone in need, help me to be an intercessor for them, even if they are not currently in my life. Speak their name to me Lord in such a miraculous way that I cannot doubt that it is an immediate instruction from you. Give me a heart of obedience to go into prayer according to your timing for them. I know that delayed obedience is disobedience. Let not disobedience have any place in my life. I thank you Lord, in advance for every deliverance and healing that you are sending now and in the future in the name of Jesus. May your will be done in each of their lives.

In Jesus Name, I Pray. Amen

SIX

HE NEEDS YOU MORE THAN YOU KNOW

consider this chapter to be very important because it also focuses on keeping the peace in your marriage and protecting your spouse's mind. This chapter focuses on how a wife can help her husband balance things in his life and help him to have peace in the mist of any storm he may be going through. The words here are written to help couples understand how much they need each other to balance things out. Satan is always lurking and looking for his next victim(s) to attack and it is usually the married household because he hates unity. If he can cause division of any sort in your household, he uses that to build his playhouse, all while he is in the mist of tearing yours down. I have learned that people tend to criticize what they do not understand and most people who are not grounded in God's word tend to judge and criticize those who are and living by it. A woman/wife was created to be a man's helpmate and that means she is the help to with what he is missing or needs throughout his life and in their marriage. A woman of God understands that protecting those that God allows to come into her life brings meaning and purpose. She understands that her husband needs her nurturing nature when he has experienced a loss or when things are not going as planned. He needs her support. She knows that in order to build that home on a solid foundation it must be built on the word of God. The woman of God is aware that her husband needs her prayers of protection and guidance from God in order to properly lead their household. God wants us to model our lives according to his word. Proverbs 31:10 says that "Charm is deceptive, and beauty is fleeting; but a woman who fears the LORD is to be praised." If we could do it on our own there would be no need for prayer. We need God to intervene in our relationships because He knows us, and our spouses better than we do. When we think we have everything figured out and we try to do things our own way, we find ourselves in the mist of chaos and destruction in our lives. The divorce rate is much higher in the world today because in many cases there is a mate in the household who is trying to dominate the other instead making the marriage a partnership. When this happens, it feels like a race to the finish line for the grand prize that no one gets in the end. A woman is not supposed to be dominate over the man she is there to submit to him, meaning she is there to help. God created man first and then the woman because she was created to help him not to control him. If we look around us today, we see more women dying of heart attacks and strokes than ever before. I believe the reason for this is because women today are trying to take on the role as the leader of the home and that means she has no room for anything else because she is taking on another role in the home she was never created for. This does not mean that a woman does not have the right to work. There are women in the bible who also worked but taking care of everything and being too independent can cause a woman to lose sight of what is important and lose her own identity in the mist of it. When a man hears a woman say, "I don't need you, I can do it by myself" that is a red flag for him. No man wants to stay where he is not needed. It makes him feel less than a man when he has no role to play in your life. This is the reason we hear so many women say, "He left me for her, and I was paying all the bills". He did not leave you for her but instead he left for a peace of mind. He went where he felt he was needed. A man is a man when he handles responsibilities. Strong marriages and relationships are built on couples needing one another and understanding the duty that one another has in the marriage. This understanding is particularly important not just for the couple but for the children involved too. For example, no one wants their child to grow up and take care of everything in the marriage by themselves. I always say that a woman can raise a boy, but she cannot teach him how to be a man. The reason for this is because men and women think totally different and vice versa a man cannot teach his daughter how to be a woman only a mother can do that. God designed it that way so that it would be the only way to balance everything out. I know that some people reading this might not agree but take a minute and look around you, study the patterns of others to see how these roles fit into their lives. A woman can train or teach her son how she would like for a man to treat her, and man can only teach his daughter what characteristics to look for in a man. There is a big difference. These two roles were never intended to be mixed up, that is why it is important for both parents to establish a strong foundation for their children relationship as well. History tends to repeat itself unless you both are willing to do the work to make the necessary changes. If not, that very same history will show up again and again in generations to come. The cycle will not stop. Your spouse needs you more than you know. You are his support and his peace. When the world around him is filled with chaos, he turns to you to be his peace. A man's peace is one of the most important things in his life. It is one of the ways that you, as his helpmate protects him by helping him have a peace of mind. If a man does not find peace in his own home, he will find every reason not to be there. This is not the will of God for your marriage. One of the main reasons the virtuous woman is spoken so highly of in Proverbs 31:10-31 is because of the way she runs her household. I will not get into all the characteristics of the virtuous woman, but I will say that she understands that putting God first and leaning on him to guide her and help her keep it all together is very important. In order to keep the peace in our household we must understand the foundation of marriage is built on God's word and doing things his way. The bible says in Proverbs 27:16 that it is better for a man to be on the roof top than in the house with a quarrelsome wife.

Basically, what this bible verse is stating is that your husband should not come home to you fussing about something all the time. I'm not saying that you should be silent about a matter, what I am saying is when you speak to him about a matter and you cannot come to a solution to the problem right away, instead of continuing to fuss and complain about it, take it to God in prayer. I have learned that when you pray over a matter and ask God the best way to handle it, he not only guides you on how to handle the matter and what to say, he works on the other person as well. You see when we pray about something that concerns us and someone close to us (such as our spouse) God knows that what affects them also affects us as well. When we allow arguments and silent treatment to get out of hand or we do not handle them the way God wants us to, it creates chaos instead of peace in the household and this is the perfect entry way for Satan to slide in through the back door. Do not let this happen to your marriage. Start today by using prayer and being obedient to God's word as your weapon. The prayer of the righteous are heard and answered. Take your position now and stand in faith on God's word knowing that you two can conquer anything together.

PRAYER FOR YOUR HUSBAND

Heavenly Father, I come to you now on behalf of my marriage. I ask you Lord to show me the correct way (according to your will) how to be the virtuous wife my husband needs me to be. I know that creating a peaceful home for him to come home to is very important not just for us, but also for our children. Help us to always be understanding of one another's needs and give us the knowledge and strength of how to meet those needs. Give us understanding of any unspoken emotions so that we can help heal each other of any hurts. Heavenly Father, as of right now, I pray for an immediate hedge of protection around my marriage to (say your spouse's name). Let no one or nothing ever be able to penetrate this hedge of protection around us. I also pray for a hedge of protection around everyone in our household so that no demonic force can come against any of us to cause destruction or harm in our children's lives as well. Lord help my husband to be the man you created him to be so that he can lead our home properly according to your will and purpose for our lives. Send your angels to keep watch over him in all his ways so that no harm or danger will come his way (Psalm 91:11). Help him to always hear your voice and to be obedient to your will. Allow him to see that any other voice in our marriage (other than yours Lord) will cause division in our home. Remind us daily to never let the sun go down on our anger towards one another but instead to talk things out and come together in prayer about any disagreements. We know that staying angry is not of you but a trick of the devil to cause us to become bitter and resentful towards one another. I pray that we will always be mindful of each other's feelings and make the necessary apologies in order to fix the situation. In you Lord is the peace that passes all understanding (Philippians 4:7). Remove anyone from our lives who may be tempted to cause destruction in our marriage, no matter who they are. When we took those vows, we became one in your sight so I ask that help us to keep ungodly friends, meddlesome in laws and those who will tempt us to get into sin, away from us and out of our marriage. We know that bad company corrupts good manners (1 Corinthians 15:33). Give us insight on how to sever friendships with anyone who is or will be bad company for either of us. I also ask that you give us the right words to speak to each together when we don't feel right about something knowing that it is a warning sign from the Holy Spirit that something is not of your will. May we both set our pride aside and be humble enough to heed the advice given by the other and take it you in prayer for confirmation. Bring other God-fearing married couples into our lives for us to pray for and pray with so that both our marriages will be strengthen in our walk with you. In your word, you said "What God hath joined together let not man take asunder" (Mark 10:9) may we always stand on your word knowing that nothing and no one can come against us because you are the third cord that keeps us tied together (Ecclesiastes 4:12). Thank you, Lord, for bringing us together and being the solid foundation that our marriage is built on. We trust you with our lives Lord and from this day forward may me and my household continue to worship and serve you for the rest of our lives. May we always be covered by the blood of the Lamb.

In Jesus Name I pray. Amen

SEVEN

SHE NEEDS YOU MORE THAN YOU KNOW

This section is written to husbands help you to get a better understanding of what is going on with your wife that she may not be speaking. There are many women who have trouble communicating how they really feel out of fear that their husband will not understand or even try to be considerate of what they are going through. The bible commands a husband to love his wife (Ephesians 5:25) and a wife to respect her husband (1 Peter 3:1). Husbands, please understand this, a wife will willing submit to you if you are allowing God to be the head of your life. A man that is following God is easier to follow because he knows where is going. Men are called to be the head and lead, but this becomes a problem when the man has no direction of where he's going. Following a man that is not following God is like the blind leading the blind, both will fall into the ditch (Matthew 15:14). This is a very scary thing in the eyes of a wife led by a man with no direction. Remember you two are one, so this affects you both. Your wife wants to feel that when you must decide something, you will consider how it will affect everyone in the household. Her thought is one wrong decision made by her husband out of fear or selfishness can destroy everything the two of you have built together. This is one of the fearful thoughts that flows through her mind. She wants to know that you will do everything within reason to protect her physically, spiritually, mentally and financially. She wants to feel that what the two of you have is secure and it is built on a solid foundation. She knows there are temptations of all sorts that you may experience in the world, but she wants the security of knowing that she can trust you to stay faithful and walk away from it no matter what it is. Yes, this too works both ways, but in many cases a woman who truly loves her husband and is allowing God to guide and lead her life, she knows her strength is in the Lord, and he will deliver her from temptation. A good wife will honor her vows and honor the king in you if you show her the love and appreciation, she deserves from you. When your wife knows how much you appreciate her and the things, she does to keep your household in order, she will go far and beyond what is required of her. Noone wants to stay somewhere where they feel broken, sad or unappreciated. This normally happens in marriages where the husband is constantly cheating which in result makes her feel that she's not good enough for him. In other instances, the husband maybe very controlling making her feel that she does not have a voice in the marriage. God never intended for the man to dominate the woman or the woman to dominate the man, but instead the woman help the man. The wife is there to be helpmate that helps you bring it all together and she will willing do this in many cases if she feels loved and accepted by you. Most men are unsure of how to show their wife she is still loved and appreciated often because society puts emphasis on special holidays like birthdays, Valentine's Day, Mother's Day and Christmas. Don't get me wrong, women love that these holidays do exist, and it means a lot for a husband to take out the time to recognize these important occasions, but she also wants to know that she is stilled love the other three hundred and sixty-one days of the year. In order to ensure this love is carried out in a way she can clearly see and feel it, affection must be shown. Affection is one way to show her that she is the center of your world, and she feels that empty place that is there when she is not around. She wants to be ensured that the love and affection she desires is just as important to you as it is to her. She wants to feel you hold her and tell her lets pray about this together and let God reveal to us what is the best way to handle this situation. When your wife knows that she can run home to you when she has had a long day at work or someone rude has cut her off in traffic. You are there ready to greet her with a kiss and tell that everything is going to be alright. Your actions towards her will not only have a positive effect on her but also the children and other family members who are watching and observing you two. Whether you husbands believe it or not, in-laws will normally treat your wife by the way they see you treat her. If you treat your wife with much care and respect, it means you value her. It shows them how much of a positive effect she has on your life and how she helps you to be a better person. This shows your family that she has your best interest at heart, and what mother does not want that for her son. This is also shining a positive light on your mom showing that she raised a wise respectable man. Proverbs 15:20 states that "A wise son brings joy to his father, but a foolish son brings grief to his mother" so as you can see the decisions you make even in your marriage and household still affects those around you. The way you treat your wife in front of your kids and other will also determine the future spouse for your children. Everything in the life not only affect us, but it also affects the generations that come after us. If you are caring and loving to your wife, these are characteristics that your daughter will look for in her future husband. On the other hand, if you are angry, mean and cheating all the time, get ready for your son-in-law to be a reflection of you. This works for the sons also; they will treat their wives how they see you treat their mother. Children tend to repeat the behavior that they have witnessed for a long period of time. Proverbs 22:6 says "Train up a child in the way they shall go and when they are old, they will not depart from it" meaning that whatever you show and teach them in their years growing up is what they will do when they get older. Your children should never witness anything you do not want to see manifested in them. The best way to ensure peace and happiness in your marriage is to keep it covered in prayer and always let God be the light that guides you down the path you should take, so that you can lead properly. It will be the solution to any problem the two of you face because you will know that you are walking in obedience and that third voice in your marriage will be God's voice and no one else's. If you have not been praying about your marriage and your wife's needs individually, it is not too late to start now. God can change the hearts and minds of the both of you and restore whatever is missing and bring that joy back again. God rejoices in Unity. Satan parties where there is division; do not give him any room to celebrate. May God bless your union from this day forward as you now start to cover your wife in prayer.

PRAYER FOR YOUR WIFE

Heavenly Father I come to you in the name of Jesus, I ask that you give me the wisdom and knowledge I need to lead my household according to your will. I realize that for my wife to respect me and trust me to make the right decisions in our marriage, I must allow you to be the head of my life. Help me to never allow my pride to get in the way of my decision making but to pray about them first and allow you to reveal to me what the answer should be. May we always be open and honest with one another about what is troubling us so that we can work together to find a solution to the problem. Give her the courage to always be open with me about what concerns her or is troubling her heart. Give me the wisdom to find ways to help her heal from things that may have broken her in the past and help her to do the same for me. I pray that your peace will always reign in our household. Lord, break any soul ties she may have from previous relationships and may those tormenting memories fade away as I strive daily to be the husband, she needs me to be. May the new memories we make as a family fill any emptiness those past wombs have created. I ask you Heavenly Father to reveal to me new and creative ways to shower her with affection so that she will know how much I love her. Help me to balance everything and make her my priority over everything else. Lord, I ask that you cover my wife with your Shield of protection (Psalm 91) so that no harm will come her way. Keep her safe wherever she goes and in whatever she does. Give me the spirit of discernment (1 Corinthians 2:14) provided by your Holy Spirit Lord, to know when she is in danger, or something is not right in my spirit so that I can immediately cover her in prayer. Your word says, "Be sober, be vigilant because your adversary Satan is lurking like a roaring lion looking for whom he may devour" (1 Peter 5:8). Do not let my wife be a victim of his evil tactics. I now ask that you also place a hedge of protection around her and our children according to Job 1:10. Allow this hedge of protection to always be in place so that no satanic attack will be able to hurt or harm her in any way. I thank you Heavenly Father that no weapon formed against her, our marriage or household will prosper according to your word in (Isaiah 54:17). I thank you Lord for showing favor in my life by sending me to find the wife you created for me. May you continue to bless our union all the days of our lives. Let nothing and no one separate what you have joined together under your divine covenant (Mark 10:9). May your name and works be glorified daily as we strive to do your will.

In Jesus Name I Pray, Amen.

EIGHT

YOUR MOST PRECIOUS
GIFT IS YOUR CHILDREN

Children are the most precious gift we can receive other than life itself. The bible says that "Children are a heritage from the LORD, offspring a reward from him" (Psalm 127:3). They are the most innocent, honest humans you ever want to meet; God made them that way. His plans have always been and always will be for good and not for evil (Jeremiah 29:11). Therefore, it is important that we raise our children in the right the way so when they are older, they will remember what they were taught and will stick to it. Proverbs 22:6 explains this so that we can understand that this is God's will for the lives of our children, and we can definitely see good results from doing this. I felt the need to place this verse here because just as we as adults face the attacks of Satan and his evil forces, our children do too. Satan knows those that are most precious to us, are also most precious to God and that is why he targets the children of God. Our children are in a battle every day to become who God created them to be or who Satan wants them to be. You may not realize it yet by just looking on the surface of things because Satan works through deception, deceiving others. As a parent you have the authority over him through prayer. I am a firm believer that parents feel things before they happen because your children are a part of you. I honestly believe God give parents this instinct about their children so that they can pray to him so that any plans of evil against their children will not prevail by any means. With the advancement of technology today, children are exposed to more peer pressure to do things that are not pleasing in God's eyes, but that is Satan's plan. As a parent, you must always be watchful about this. I am not saying quit your job and sit at the computer with them or hang out with them and their friends at the mall each time they are out of your sight. Just do not ignore any gut feeling you may have that something

63

is wrong. I have found that whether you realize it or not, parents you are your children's first role

model. Have you ever noticed your children repeating something you said, or you find them mimicking something you did in front of them without realizing it? This is because they look up to you. I'm sure that once or twice in your lifetime you have heard a little girl say, "I'm going to be like my mom when I grow up" or a little boy say, "I'm going to be like my dad when I grow up." This works for children who are adopted as well as aunts and uncles who end up raising children like their own. Parents are born leaders to their children that is why it is important to lead them in the right way when they are younger. We never stop learning even as adults so of course our children are constantly watching and learning daily. Therefore, I feel that it is important for you to be who you want to see in them because they will mimic what they see. As they get older, they are exposed to so much peer pressure and persuasion from their classmates and friends on being popular, keeping up with the latest fashion trends and even drinking before the legal age. This is not what we want for our children. This is the reason why it is so important to have open and honest conversations with your children as often as possible. When they feel that they can openly talk to you about what's going on in their lives without feeling like they will be judged or will get in trouble for being around the wrong things or people. When you have a good relationship with them, it makes it harder for Satan to lure them into his will by using evil tactics. They will be aware of the evil sent out against them. Matthew 12:25 says, "A house divided against itself cannot stand" meaning that if you and your children are not on the same page, there is always going to be chaos and disorder. On the other hand, 1 Corinthians 1:10 tells us the will of the Lord, "I appeal to you brothers and sisters, in the name of the Lord Jesus Christ, that all of you agree with one another in what you say and that there be no divisions among you, but that you be perfectly united in mind and thought." God wants us to be in unity because it makes the road of parenting a little easier when you have open communication with them. Encourage your children today by letting them know that they can always come to you about anything. As you encourage them, let me encourage you to pray the following prayer for them daily. Let us not give Satan any room in the lives of our children.

PRAYER OF PROTECTION
YOUR CHILDREN

Heavenly Father, I come to you now in the name of Jesus asking that you cover my children wherever they may be at this moment. I ask that you put a Hedge of Protection around them to protect them from all harm or danger. Cancel any plans they may have that are not of your will for their lives. I cannot be everywhere they are Lord, but I know you are above all, and you see all. Nothing can happen without your permission. Even Satan had to ask you (God) for permission to attack Job (Job 1:6-12). Let him not have a place in my children's life cover them with your shield of protection and let no harm or danger come their way. Deliver them from bullies, thieves, abusers, rapist, child molesters and anyone who would have a bad influence on them. Reveal to them who their true friends are and help to be a true friend to them in return. Proverbs 27:17 says that "Iron sharpens iron; so, a man sharpens the countenance of his friend" meaning that they will have a positive influence on each other. May they always understand that in order to have friends they must always show themselves friendly and there is a friend that will stick closer than a brother (Proverbs 18:24). Help them to always have love in their hearts for others no matter their color or race. Remind them that you created all of them and they are all your children, and it brings joy to you that they live in unity with others. Lord right now, I cover my children, their friends, co-workers, bosses, teachers, classmates, principal, staff, and spouses with the Blood of Jesus and I decree and declare where the Blood of Jesus is applied, Satan and his demonic forces cannot trespass. I speak right now and cancel any plots or plans set by any demonic forces to come against them, is now null and void. Lord send your angels to guide, protect and to lead each of them back home safely. Help them to see your light shining on the path they are to take so that no evil will happen to them (Psalm 91:10). I pray that you will keep them safe and guide them in the right way. Be their rock, fortress, and deliverer; the God in whom they can always trust (Psalm 18:2) knowing that you are with them no matter what.

In Jesus Mighty Name I Pray, Amen

— NINE —

DO NOT BE FOOLED...
CURSES ARE REAL

Have you ever looked around at your life or the life of someone else close to you and wonder why they keep losing things or why things are not going right no matter how hard you try? Working hard and still not able to make ends meet or get ahead? Experiencing relationship after relationship failures? Multiple miscarriages or death of children all passing away in a similar way to someone else close to you? I can ask many more questions, but I will stop at those for now. If these things are happening to you, you may be under what the bible speaks of which is a curse. A curse takes place when someone speaks or does something supernaturally evil to get the desired outcome that they want. The words we speak can bring life or death, blessings and curses (Proverbs 18:21) on ourselves and others. When a person speaks evil over others and wish them ill or even try to control or manipulate them, this is definitely not the work of God but of Satan himself. Just as well as God uses Christians (his people) to carry out his plan to lead others to Christ, the devil also has people that he works through to carry out his plan for evil to stop them from succeeding. Satan knows that in Christ, there are promises of healing, prosperity, love, peace, joy, unity, and kindness; only to name a few. It is no secret that not everyone is happy for you when you succeed or find the perfect mate that God has for you. Satan hates unity because it brings God joy to see his people united in peace. Nothing disturbs a person motivated by evil and jealousy more than seeing someone else with something they want and have not yet been able to achieve. Envy and jealousy have been a major factor in the reason why many of these things happen which are both demonic spirits. Wanting what someone else has, have led some people to use witchcraft to accomplish their goal by trying to control or manipulate the situation to work in their favor.

There are people who have passed away and never walked in their purpose because someone else was controlling and manipulating their mind to keep them trapped in a situation going nowhere for their lives. This is selfish and inconsiderate, and it is certainly not God's will for anyone's life. The bible says in Deuteronomy 18:10-11, "There shall not be found among you anyone who makes his son or daughter pass through the fire [as a sacrifice], one who uses divination and fortune-telling, one who practices witchcraft, or one who interprets omens or a sorcerer or one who casts a charm or spell, or a medium, or a spiritualist, or a necromancer [someone who seeks to communicate with the dead]". It further goes on to say, "For all who does these things are an abomination to the LORD: and because of these abominations, the Lord thy God doth drive them out from before you" -Deuteronomy 18:12. As you can see God is not pleased with this at all. Matthew 6:24 clearly says that you cannot serve two masters because you will love one of them and hate the other one. When you are practicing witchcraft and speaking curses (your will) on the lives of others, you are worshiping idols that are not of God, our Heavenly Father. Anything that does not allow a person to make their own choices is a form of witchcraft and control. God gives every individual here on earth free will because he wants you to have a choice of whom you want to serve. He does not want you to feel like you are being forced to do anything that will not bring you joy which is an important fruit of the spirit. This why it is explained in Joshua 24:14-15 that is it was undesirable to the people to serve the LORD, the Living God then it was stated "Choose now for yourselves whom you will serve, whether it is the gods of your forefathers (ancestors) beyond the river or the gods of the Amorites, in whose land you are living" either way they had to make a choice. Joshua made it clear that him and his house would serve the Lord because he knew the consequences that for came with following other gods. There is never any good that comes from following and cherishing anything that is not of God. God blesses us with the desires of our heart as rewards for our obedience to him but, if you get in a hurry and decide you are going to take these things by force, you will never experience the joy and happiness the real thing came bring. You will have the artificial version of what God really wanted you to have and anything artificial or fake eventually withers and fades away. In some cases, people are born into curse through no fault of their own, this is when their parents' ancestors were in a direct lineage of a curse or they worship other gods which put them under a curse, this passed down for many generations. Examples of this can be as I stated earlier multiple miscarriages of the womb, men or women in the family who never marry or family history of divorce, constant financial problems no matter how much money that person makes, it's never enough for them to get ahead. Something unexpected always comes up to make them have to spend the extra money they thought they would have to get ahead. The good news in all of this is there is a solution these problems. No curse can stay on a person walking right with God meaning that if your heart is right and you are obedient to what God tells you to do, He will take those very same curses and turn them into blessings (Nehemiah 13:2) because he loves you just that much. He wants to see you succeed and his will carried out in your life not what someone else's ill wishes for your life. Prayer changes circumstances and turns things around while praising him makes the enemy flee. I have found that it's hard to do one without the other because when I pray, I feel a joy deep inside of me that rises up and makes me want to praise God for the already answered prayers and the ones that are to come. The more you worship him, pray and communicate with him, you will see how much your joy will increase and anything that was hindering you through no fault of your own will be lifted, curses broken, doors will open, and the right opportunities will knock. If it is bad relationships, prayer can break that curse so that the husband or wife that God has hand-picked for you can be found by you (if you are a man) or you will be found (if you are a woman) by the man. When you are obedient, God has a way of sending you what you desire in a way that you will have to admit that only He could have made it happen that way. God does things differently. He says "Remember not the former things, nor consider the things of old. Behold, I will do a new thing" (Isaiah 43:18-19). Never think that you know how or when God is going to do something because He does it differently and unexpected. On other hand, Satan works with the familiar. He does not have the power God has so he will keep sending you a replica of what he knows you like. It will be the generic version of what God truly has for you like the same pattern of people you have dated in the past or a job opportunity you always wanted opens up but the plant is headed for bankruptcy six months from now so no one there will have a job. Satan does not care that you do not have the finances in six months to take care of your household. His purpose is to get you distracted and off track so that you will give up on your purpose and never succeed. It is time to break curses and crush Satan under your feet. No matter how things may look, never despair because God has a time for everything to take place. Trust his timing and stay in faith as you pray.

PRAYER TO BREAK AND
DESTROY CURSES

Heavenly Father, In the Mighty Name of Jesus I ask that you break any curses of witchcraft, manipulation and control, generational curses and any unknown spoken word curses that have been placed on me or on _____'s life. Lord, let any witchcraft and manipulation done to control our minds and lives be exposed and destroyed. I decree and declare right now that it has no power over our lives, or the life of anyone else connected to us. We are now completely free of any bondages and strongholds placed on our lives by these demonic forces. Clear our minds of any wrong thinking caused by this course of action. Heavenly Father, I pray that any wrong decisions that we have made due to witchcraft and wrong curses being placed on us will no longer have a negative effect on our lives. We are looking to you Lord to bring good out of all of it. Your word says in Genesis 50:20, that they meant it for evil, but you Lord meant it for good. Destroy the work of witchcraft in their hands. May they no longer be allowed to cast spells on others according to your word stated in Micah 5:12. I pray that anyone involved in bringing these curses to pass will be exposed and brought to the light. Help them to realize that doing evil and causing others to stumble only leads to hell and destruction. Remind them that those who are not of you but choose to serve idols will burn in the Lake of Fire for eternity. Help them to understand "When you stretch out your hand, those who are helping will fall and those who are hoping will fall and they all shall fall together" Isaiah 31:3. Don't let evil plans succeed in my life or _____'s life. I decree and declare that right now your will and your will only will be done in my life and _____'s life on earth as it is in heaven. We know that your will is not that anyone shall perish but be brought to repentance (2 Peter 3:9). Give them a chance to repent of their evil ways before they go away and be no more. Help us to forgive them so that we will be forgiven for our sins. Enable us to let go of any hurts and bitterness this may have caused in our lives. Lord turn these curses into blessings (Nehemiah 13:2) for us and everyone associated with these curses have affected because I know you love us, and you want what's best for each of our lives. Lord, I thank you for breaking and destroying these curses and yolks of bondage placed on our lives. May the healing and blessing process begin now in the Mighty Name of Jesus.

In Jesus Name I Pray, Amen

TEN

YOUR MARRIAGE IS UNDER ATTACK

This chapter is very dear to my heart because marriage brings amazing results when the two people involved are dwelling together in unity. Marriage is a special covenant designed by God to help one another become all that He designed them to be. When you are with the person that God created you to be with, there will be a sense of peace that takes place when you the two of you meet. God will reveal things to the both of you that will help you build a solid foundation that no one can destroy. He will help you both to communicate in ways that others may not be able to comprehend or understand. You will understand what's going on with your spouse/ mate because as you pray God will reveal it. The reason this happens is because whatever the qualities that are missing in you, they are hidden in your spouse. God designed the two of you to balance each other out. Therefore it's important to marry equally yoked because your spouse will play a big role in fulfilling the purpose God has for your life. For example, if you are a wife, your husband may own a body shop painting and repairing cars. He doesn't have the time, or the mind set to balance the books, order the parts and take inventory at the same time. It is only 24 hours in a day the shop is open eight of them. This is where you come in as his helpmate to help balance it out. You may have the time and enjoy sitting at a desk creating invoices, counting inventory and ordering parts. This will also create a peaceful atmosphere for him to work in because he knows he can trust you and you will do him no harm. The bible says that the Proverbs 31-Woman's husband trust her knowing that she will do good by him. Everyone wants to be with someone that will be honest, caring and most of all, honor their vows. When two people take those vows before God, a covenant is created, and those promises are meant to be carried out until one or both take their last breath is taken. I know couples who have been married for years and I can honestly say they are genuinely happy with one another even though their children are grown now with families of their own. There are a few things I have found to be true in these marriages. One of them is to never go to bed anger with one another. The bible says do not let the sun go down and you are still angry (Ephesians 4:26). When you go to bed angry with your spouse, you are going to wake up angry with your spouse and if it is not soon dealt with and repented of, it is going to take root in you and cause you to become mean and bitter. This gives Satan a place in your marriage in which it leads to more strife and one of you are sleeping in the kid's old room. Secondly, I have realized that married couples who put God first in their marriage are more understanding and considerate of each other. In cases such as these, the wife understands that submitting to the leading of her husband keeps her under the covering of his protection. She understands that respecting her husband is part of her role as a wife and it not only blesses them, but it pleases the Lord also. The husband knows that his role is to lead his household, and this means he must know where he is going. He knows without God's direction he is headed for a dead-end road, and he does not want that for his family. A man of God knows that for his wife to respect him and follow his lead, she must be able to trust the decisions he makes. On the other hand, you have the man that is not led by God and makes unwise or foolish decisions that brings hardship and challenges. This type of husband makes it hard for the wife to submit (no matter much she prays) because he has no sense of direction about where he is going. This is very, dangerous because Satan will send all forms of deception, luring him into temptation of all sorts. When this happens, the marriage will normally end in divorce sometime later because without God there is no knowledge and strength to control the fleshly desires. When two individuals marry, two flesh become one so what affects one person, affects the other. God loves unity; Satan likes division. I'm sure you have heard the old saying "Together we stand, divided we fall" this is because you must be in agreement about anything you want to succeed in, especially marriage. The bible says a house divided cannot stand (Matthew 12:25) meaning that if the wife and husband are not in agreement and there are always signs of strife, eventually the marriage will end in divorce or the couple sleeping in separate rooms. God never intended for spouses to sleep in separate beds. The marriage bed is the only bed undefiled (Hebrews 13:4). Sleeping in separate rooms give Satan a place to play in your marriage by keeping the two of you apart. You will be amazed at the simple things he uses to get into marriages and cause destruction. He knows the strength of two far outweighs the strength of one. That is why it so very important for both spouses to do their part in the marriage to keep it in tack. It is easier to keep Satan out of your marriage, than it is to kick him out once he is in your marriage. You and your spouse have the authority over Satan and through prayer you are equipped to stand against any attacks he attempts to send your way. Prayer brings peace of mind, knowing that God will weather the storm and bring you out together peacefully. There is no amount of money you can place on having a peace of mind or your marriage. It is a beautiful thing, and you get to share it with the beautiful person God created just for you.

DEFENSE PRAYER FOR
MARRIED COUPLES

This prayer is meant to be joined and prayed together by both spouses. "Again, I say unto you, that if two of you shall agree on earth touching anything that they shall ask, it shall be done for them of my Father which is in Heaven." -Matthew 18:19. Heavenly Father we come before you now with a praise on our lips and gratefulness in our hearts. We praise you for who you are and the things you have done throughout our lives. We thank you Lord for sending us each other. Our marriage has proven to be one of the greatest rewards for our obedience to you. There is no greater gift than love. May our love for you and each other increase daily as we walk this journey together. Give us spiritual eyes to see the hidden attacks set by Satan so that we will not fall into them. We ask that you order both of our steps and that you will remove temptation from our lives. Whenever we are tempted to do or say something that we should not, allow your Holy Spirit to speak to us that it is not of your will for our lives so that we will not do anything we will later regret. Remind us that there are consequences for our actions. Help us to always respect each other, be honest with one another and to be mindful of each other's feelings so that we will not give Satan an entrance to cause division in our marriage through anger or deception. Give us the desire for only each other and no one else so we will remain faithful to each other thereby giving no room for the spirit of lust and adultery. We ask that as we age, we become more beautiful and handsome to each other so that we will always remember why we said those vows to each other on our wedding day. Give us wisdom to always consider each other before making any decisions that will affect our household. If there comes a time that we are not in agreement about what the right decision is, remind us to come to you in prayer trusting and believing that the truth will be revealed. Show us anything in our home that is not of you and can hinder our prayers from being answered. We want what you want for our lives. Only you know what is best for the two of us. We look to you to unveil ways that we can help, honor and support one another in our purposes. We know amazing things happen when we serve and support each other. Help us to always keep you as the head of our marriage as we strive daily to make each other the top priority in our lives. Keep us knowledgeable of what one another is feeling so that we can find ways to bring joy where there is sadness, healing where there is sickness, peace where there is chaos and assurance where there is uncertainty. Place our vows as a seal on our hearts and minds as a reminder that no matter how tough things may get or how good certain moments may be, we married each other for better and for worse. Only you can help us keep this promise to you and to one another. Take any thoughts of divorce away from us knowing that there is always a solution to the problem and divorce should never be the answer. Remind the both of us that divorce not only affects us, but our children and other family members as well. Help us to realize that this is a strategy of Satan to divide two families with whom you have joined. Do not let that happen Lord. Strengthen us daily as we walk with you and continue to strive to make one another happy. May we always communicate with one another so that we will remain on the same page. Bring into our lives other married, trustworthy Christian couples with whom we can pray and do things with so that both marriages will be strengthened. Help us to learn from one another so that we all can grow in you Lord. Proverbs 27:17 says, "Iron sharpens iron, so a man sharpens the countenance of his friend" help us to have this impact on our friends and vice versa. Give us knowledge of when something is wrong in their marriage so that we can immediately bring their marriage together in prayer so that the spirit of division will have no place in their lives. We trust our friendships, lives and marriages to you Lord and ask that your will be done in them.

In Jesus Name We Pray, Amen

ELEVEN

BUILDING STRONG RELATIONSHIPS WITH YOUR IN-LAWS

Joining two families together can be difficult to adjust to at first because everything is all new and everyone is getting to know each other. Building a strong relationship with your spouse's parents can contribute to a lot of his or her peace. Whenever there is tension among you and your spouse's parents, it makes them feel like they are being faced with a choice of who to agree with leaving them sad and disappointed. I know that some relationships can be difficult if the other person shows selfish and stubborn ways but if the bible says, "Be not overcome with evil, but overcome evil with good" (Romans 12:21). As a child of the Most High God, He expects us to be peacemakers and to do good to those in spite of the way they react to us. I have personally experienced situations where individuals have been rude to me upon meeting the first time but as I continued to be nice and caring, they changed the attitude. We must realize that when a person is mean or bitter towards you, it has nothing to do with you, but it has more to do with something in their life that has brought them pain and they are still holding on to that hurt. When things hurt us or our children, we tend to put up a wall to protect ourselves and them. For example, take Naomi and Ruth's story in Ruth 1:3-21. Naomi lost both of her sons and her husband all during the time of a famine and it caused her to become bitter and anger feeling that God had let her down. She was so bitter she told others do not call her Naomi but Mara which means bitter. I can imagine the way she felt having everything and losing it all in the blink of an eye. In those moments, what she did not realize, God was still with her, and he had left her with what would appear to be the greatest gift of it all in the end. She was left with two daughters-in-law (her two son's wives) whose names were Oprah and Ruth. Naomi told them both to leave her and go start their lives somewhere else, but Ruth was not having it that way.

While Orpah took the advice and departed from Naomi, Ruth chose to stay by her side. Ruth saw the pain her mother-in-law experienced, and her caring heart would not let her walk away. She knew her mother-in-law needed her. Later in the book of Ruth, we find that Ruth also needed Naomi. As time we on, Ruth caring, and loving heart brought Naomi to find God again which led her to do away with her bitterness and resentment. The scripture does not state it, but I am sure Naomi recognized that Ruth genuinely loved her as well as her son (Obed) and she deserved to be happy. The way you treat your spouse can also play a big role in the way his or her parents treat you also. Take a moment and think about it, as a parent you want the best person for your child. You want them with someone who will take care of them like you would if they got sick. Someone who will make decisions based on what is best for the both of you (not operating in selfish motives). No parent wants to worry about if their adult child is going to be safe with the person they chose to marry. The way you treat a person is always the reflection of the way you see yourself. God wants us to treat everyone with love and respect. I am not saying that you must stick around someone who is constantly verbally abusing you but, what I am saying is, think about what things can be like if you react differently. Another important thing to factor in is that if there are children involved, these children are watching the way their parents and grandparents are acting towards each other and this can also have a negative or positive effect on them. Children watch everything we do, and they will begin to treat a person the way they see us treat them. So, if you and your mother-in-law or father-in-law are bickering at the dinner table every Sunday, then they are not going to respect their grandparents either because they are observing the way you all are treating each other. This too can be extremely dangerous because this can be carried down generation after generation. I try to always keep this forefront of my mind because what I do today determines what my children will do tomorrow. I am a firm believer that it is easier to be nice to someone than it is to be rude. Being rude to someone is draining and it leaves you in a bad mood, thinking about the offense continuously. It is much easier to be nice. Being nice to someone leaves you with joy and peace of mind knowing you did the right thing. My advice to everyone engaged and married already is that when you pray for your spouse and children, also include a prayer in there for your in-laws. Praying for them will help God to open their eyes and change their hearts for the better. In the meantime, he will also work on your heart so that you will be able to see the changes they are making and not hold their past offences against them as they are working to change. Allowing God to work on you both to help you build a stronger relationship can be rewarding in ways you can never imagine. This in return will bring great rewards on both sides. There is no way to put a price on your spouse's happiness but can be one of the greatest rewards you can give them is to have a peaceful relationship between you and your in-laws. This is what love is all about, wanting to see the people in your life happy. Love is about bringing joy to others and wanting to see them happy even if it means not getting your way at that time. When you love someone, you want what's best for them. There will be times you may have to sacrifice something you want to make sure they have what they need. Love is unselfish and unconditional. It does not change when circumstances change, it looks to find a solution to accommodate each other in those circumstances. When you pray, God will give the wisdom that you need to accommodate those involved. The bible says that there will be a time where a house is divided. The members of that house will be against each other, where the son against the father, father against the son, daughter against the mother, the mother against the daughter, the mother-in-law against the daughter in law. (Luke 12:51-53). This happens when someone is rebelling against the word of God. Knowing and acting on God's word brings unity, not division. This scripture shows us the danger that can happen when we do not pray and place God as the head of all our relationships. Psalm 133:1 refers to how good it is when God's people to dwell together in unity. This particular verse, it shows us how meaningful relationships can be. If you have not prayed about your relationship with your in-laws, it is not too late to start today. It brings a sense of peace to your mind when you pray about it and leave it to God to work it out on your behalf. He can restore and repair any damage that may have been done already. He is a God of rewards and restoration. Allow him to do that in your life and theirs. It will take your marriage to a greater level of peace that you may not have known existed. God has the power to do that. Trust him today with your relationships. When we pray for others, God shines a light on the best way to handle the situation. Always seek Him for the answers and wait with expectation.

RELATIONSHIP PRAYER FOR IN-LAWS

Heavenly Father, I call on you now and ask that you intervene in my relationship with my in-laws. It is my desire to that we have a mother daughter relationship and father and son relationship. I realize that when my spouse and I got married, we became one in your sight but we each also gained another set of parents. I ask that you strengthen our relationships with our parents and in-laws. I know that my in-laws play a big role in my spouse's life and now that I am a part of his/her life, they will play a big role in mine. Help us to always treat each other with respect. Help us to always be understanding of one another's feelings. May we always set good examples for our children so that they will always honor and respect their grandparents. Your word says that "Children's children are a crown to their grandparents" (Proverbs 17:6) help us to never keep our children from their grandparents because of selfish reasons. Give us the wisdom to settle any disagreements we may have with our parents and in-laws so that no bitterness and resentment will take root in any of our hearts. I also pray that both of our parents will be loving and understanding to one another realizing that they also have a big effect on the way our children are raised as well. Help them to be understanding of that rules we set for our children are to protect them. May they not judge, criticize or violate those rules in order to gain favor with our children. May we always agree when a decision must be made about our children. I know that grandparents can sometimes give into temper tantrums, but I ask that you give them wisdom to handle the situation with our children as it arises. Remind us (my spouse and myself) to never discuss any difficulties in our marriage with our parents knowing that this can cause division and disunity. I also pray that our parents will understand and respect our decision to never discuss matters about our marriage with them. May they understand that we are adults and any problems we may have should be handle between the two of us. Your word reminds us that we left or parents and became one so that means we must find a way to resolve our problems between the two of us. Help of us (myself and my spouse) to always be mindful of the words we speak about each other in front of our parents and others. Remind us that it can a positive or negative effect on the way they treat them. It is my desire that your love will reign in each of our hearts and that we all can work together to always built each other up and not tear each other down. Bring us together to pray for one another so that we can know the peace and unity it brings. We know that a family standing together can weather any storm. Help us to be that family. I thank you Lord for working out your peace and understanding in each of our lives. As we gather as a family, remind each of us to never take each other for granted.

In Jesus Name, Amen

TWELVE

LETTING GO,
THE FINAL GOODBYE

Sometimes letting go can be the hardest thing to do. There are times when God tells us to let something go because that something in our life has ended but the prideful side of our human nature wants to hold on refusing to let it go. We hold on to memories, friendships and relationships and material possessions. We even hold on to the hope that the very things we are holding on to that God will breathe life back in it and restore it to its original state. We do these things out of fear of starting over. The fact that we have invested so much time and effort in it and even the negative thoughts of "You failed" began to rise because it didn't work out. I have found out that the key to happiness is letting go of the hope that God will change his mind about something He has showed or told us to let go. When God tells us to let something go, we tend to want to hold on a little tighter to it thinking that if God starts to see that this is something that I really want and I know this is best for me, He will change his mind, or the other person(s) involved in the situation. It does not work that way. In Psalm 37:4, when it says He will give you the desires of your heart, you must trust that He will, but in his own way and time. His will and his way are always different from ours because he knows what makes us sad today will also be the very thing that will destroy us 10 years from now. It is impossible to move on to something new if you are still holding on to something old. Nothing new begins until something old ends and you must let some old things go in order to make room for something new. For example, most people who want a new car, they never attempt to go get it until the old car stops and never cranks up again. In this case, you are forced to let it go. This is what happens with most of the things in our lives. When you are praying about something, you must be prepared to let go of what was and walk toward what will be. When you continue to hold on to what use to be, you find yourself running back to what was, out of fear of change. Change is always uncomfortable but if you are moving in the center of God's will the outcome is always worth it. He will never guide you into something that He is not in himself, but this only happens when you are willing to say "yes" to his will for your life. I can recall some time ago in my life when God spoke to me about leaving everything I had behind and not looking back. For a while, I kept saying I got to get some new stuff before I can get rid of the stuff I already have. But I felt in my spirit that God wanted me to let it all go and start over. As I continued to pray for the direction God wanted me to take in my life, He continued to speak to me through scriptures, feelings of discomfort, unsafety in the place I was in and even signs through television. It was like the pastor was speaking directly to me. I would sometimes wonder how they knew my thoughts (with a slight smile), but I knew it was God speaking through those various people to get a message to me. If there is one thing, I have found to be true about an instruction from God is that you cannot run from it no matter how you try. You will continue to go around in the same circle not accomplishing anything until you say, "Yes Lord, I will do it your way." Although I wanted to be obedient to the Lord, I still had that part in me that wanted to help him out a little by having a backup plan of my own. Let me be the first to tell you, it did not work. God made my circumstances so uncomfortable for me until I reached a point in my life to say, "Lord, wherever you want me to be and whatever you want me to do, I will do it." I am ready to say yes to your will. The instructions came back to be again, "Sell all that thou hast and give to the poor and follow me" which came through by scripture (Luke 18:22 KJV). I did just that and once I did, the answer came as to why I had to do things this way. I realized that God saw the memories that these possessions held for me were daily destroying me and if I got new things, it would have been similar to the old items because I had not changed my mindset. You see it was only when I started to pull things out, (one by one) I realized that the memories I had with each of these items were link to something or someone that was taken away from me I loved dearly. It was in that moment when I realized that the sadness and depression was stemming from what I was looking at every day. I started with my clothes and work my way around to the last picture on the wall. In order to change my life, I had to change my mindset first. I struggled a lot with letting go of the memories of losing my loved ones and I think the most recent at the time of me giving everything up was, my losing my niece. She died a tragic death and getting that phone call to go and check things out replayed over and over in my mind from the time I sat on the couch I was sitting on when it occurred, to looking in my closet and seeing the clothes we had alike. I never knew how painful it could be keeping something in your life because of how much time you've had it or because you have memories with. It's hard to let it go, but if you don't, it will eventually destroy you. I have learned that when you let someone go in your life or they pass away, that is never the final goodbye. The final goodbye occurs when you let go of what is causing you to relive those tormenting memories. I came to understand that letting go of those things helped me to be able to think on the happy moments we shared together in which always brings a smile. My life experiences have taught me that the end of anything is always the beginning of something else. God not only instructed me to get rid of those things, but he led me in another direction leaving even my childhood home behind. He knew I daily struggled looking at the big sap tree a few yards away where my little cousin was gunned down. There was no escape for the pain, it was all around me. God knew what I needed, and he would supply everything, but I had to be obedient. I now realize you cannot have a new beginning unless you have a burial for those endings. I know now why God spoke "Don't look back, remember what happened to Lot's wife" (Luke 17:32 NIV). Start today by praying and asking God to show you what you need to let go of. What is slowly destroying you? I have provided a prayer below to get you started but make a promise to yourself, as God reveals his instructions to you that you will be willing and obedient to him no matter how much it hurts your pride to do it. "To obey is better than sacrifice" 1 Samuel 15:22. Things work out so much better when you trust and obey him. He knows and sees what we do not see, and he can do what we cannot do. Let faith take you where pride cannot.

PRAYER FOR LETTING GO

Lord, show me anything in my life from my past that I am holding on to that is hindering me from moving forward. Reveal to me any past hurts, fears, soul ties, memories, and any keepsake items or gifts that may be a hinderance to my moving forward. Heavenly Father show me how to turn my past hurts and pain into purpose so that I can be a help to others. Give me the Spirit of Joy for my mourning and beauty for my ashes (Isaiah 61:3). Send your angels to walk with me on this journey of life to protect me from any destruction that lies ahead. Protect me from depression, thoughts of suicide, and the spirit of pride which leads to destruction. Block any tormenting spirits sent out on assignment to keep me in bondage. I know that you, Heavenly Father, are the only one with the power to heal me physically and spiritually, so I ask right not in the Mighty Name of Jesus that you heal every part of my body spiritually, physically and mentally. I realize that in order to begin the healing process, I will have to let go of the things in my life that causing me to be sad and gloomy. Deliver me from those things now in the Name of Jesus. I proclaim healing throughout my mind, body and spirit. Let your Holy Spirit reign in my life now as I release all this pain and suffering to you. Heal me Lord from the top of me head to the soles of my feet. I will no longer live defeated by the enemy because the battle has already been won for me when Jesus died on the cross. Thank you, Heavenly Father, for lifting the burdens of past hurts, lies, soul ties and tormenting memories from my life. I now look forward to the new beginnings you have provided for me as I discover your will for my life. Your word says in Philippians 3:14, "I press toward the mark for the prize of the high calling of God in Christ Jesus" help me to always be mindful of this knowing that these trials are small compared to the prize that is rewarded for those who follow Jesus and stay on the path of righteousness. Lord if there is anything hidden deep inside of me from my past that Satan plans to use against me later, reveal it to me so that I can let it go and turn it over to you. I want to be free of all things that will cause me pain or hinder me in the future from moving forward into the purpose you have for me. As I take the first step to move forward with the plans you have for me, I now say my final goodbyes to sadness, loneliness, depression, anger, bitterness, past relationships, lies, tormenting memories and any other oppressive spirits seeking to weigh me down. I welcome your Holy Spirit to dwell in me as I strive daily to grow stronger in my walk with you Lord.

In Jesus Name I Pray, Amen.

CONCLUSION

I want to thank you for taking the time to read this book. I hope that it has a positive impact on everyone reading it. It is with great joy that I wrote this book knowing that it is being used to reach those around the world, who do not know me personally. I feel that it is my duty as a servant of the Lord to make sure that His word is carried out. When the Holy Spirit spoke "Go ye into all the world and preach the gospel to every creature" (Mark 16:15 KJV) my immediately thought was, "How am I supposed to do that?" "I couldn't picture myself around the world state to state, country to country preaching God's word. Writing this book has shown me that you do not have to stand up in the middle of a pulpit and preach to spread the gospel to God's people. There are so many other ways to do that. This experience has also taught me that not everyone will pick up a bible and read it and some of those who do, may not understand everything they're reading. One thing for sure, there are people who will read books that relate to their current situation because they're searching for a solution to the problem(s) they're facing. There is no better way to help someone solve their problems by giving them the advice they need along with prayer and scripture to confirm it. Writing this book has also helped me in ways I could not even imagine. It's a great feeling to know that you are doing what God has instructed you to do. I really think that it was part of God's plan all along. You're healing while helping someone else to heal at the same time. I realize that some of the trials and test I have gone through and the times of isolation from others was not only building my faith in him, but he was training me to be on the battlefield. I had to be trained to be a warrior in order to intercede and help bring His people out of the bondage that Satan has held them in for years. Never look at your trials as something terrible because God has a plan for you to help bring someone out that will be facing that similar situation. This is how God builds lasting friendships and relationships because we were never created to live in a world lost and lonely. We all need help at some point and only God can put the right people in our life to create that help. He will also move the wrong ones from our lives so that they will no longer hinder our progress. As I patiently wait for God to unveil my next move in life, I am praying for you and for everyone that receives this book. I pray that God's will be done in your life and that God's light will shine on you and your household driving out any darkness created by Satan and his demonic forces. I leave with you Love, Prayer, Faith and Peace.

Printed in the United States
by Baker & Taylor Publisher Services